S0-BZF-541

Mot Has Jam

Dad, Mom, and Kim
are on a jet.
Dad has on black slacks.

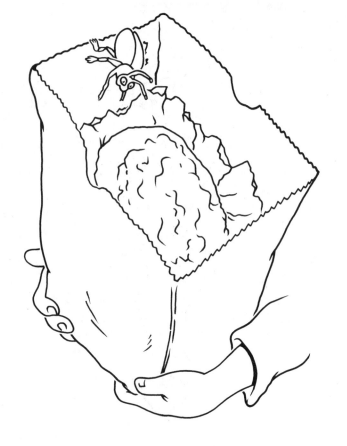

Mot, the bug, is in a sack
on the jet.
Mot wishes to have lunch
to munch.

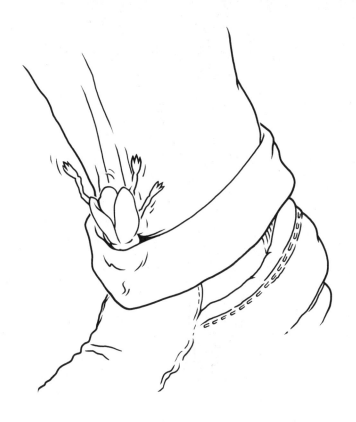

He jumps to the top
of the sack and slips.
He slips into the cuff
on Dad's slacks.

Kim has a bun with jam in it.
Kim gets her bun.
A glob of jam
falls off Kim's bun.

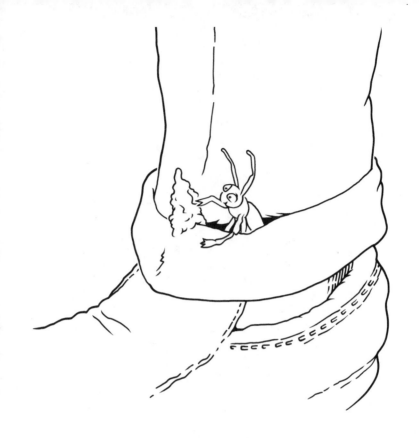

Plop! The jam slips
into Dad's cuff!
Mot is glad! Such luck!
He can munch on that
glob of jam!

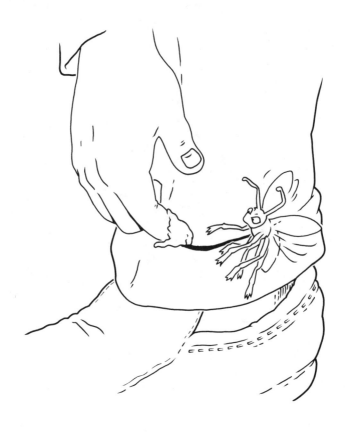

Dad plucks the jam
out of his cuff.
His hand is next to Mot!

But Dad does not get Mot.
Mot gets off Dad's cuff.
Mot is glad he had jam.

The Rash

Kim is sick.
She has a rash.
Red dots are on her back
and neck.
Red dots are on her legs
and hands.

The red rash itches.
Kim is not glad.
She is sad.
She has a big wish
to be rid of the rash.
Kim is glum.

The rash is not fun.
Kim sits on Mom's lap.
She hugs her doll.
Mom rocks Kim.
Mom's lap is soft.
Kim naps on Mom's lap.

Mom tucks Kim back in bed.
The clock ticks and Kim naps.
Kim shifts a bit.
The clock tocks
and Kim naps.
Kim gets a lot of rest.

Kim rests till she gets
her pep back.
Kim gets well.
The rash is off her back
and neck.

The rash is off
her legs and hands.
Kim is glad.
She can go to class.

She can run and hug Pam.
She can sit at her desk
next to Pam.
Kim is well.
It is bliss.

Get Fit

The Red Dogs are a club.
Get fit, Red Dogs.
Get fit to win.

Lug a big bag.
Run up the bluff.
Clip a flag to the top
of the bluff.

Get fit to win.
Rush up the hill.

Run on the logs.
Plug on, Red Dogs.
Plug on to win.

Huff and puff up the cliff.
Get fit, Red Dogs.
Get fit to win.

Do not slack off.
Do not kick back.
Plan to win.
Plot to win.
Win, Red Dogs, win!

Dress the Dolls

Kim and Pam are glum.
Plip, plop. It is wet.

The clock ticks.
The clock tocks.

Kim and Pam wish for sun.
What can they do for fun?

Pam has a plan.
Pam and Kim
will dress the dolls.
Kim claps.
Pam is glad.

Kim and Pam dress
the dolls in red and black.
Pam and Kim
chat to the dolls.

They sit and sip from cups.
Pam and Kim are glad,
not sad.

A Trip to the Vet

Kim and Gus are on
a trip to the vet.
Kim grips Gus.

Gus is not glad.
He does not wish
to go to the vet.

Gus does not wish
to have a shot.
He has a plan to trick Kim.
Gus grabs Kim's neck.

Kim drops the cat.

He runs zig-zag in the grass.

Kim runs to catch Gus.

Kim grabs Gus and
catches him.
He frets and fusses.

Kim gets Gus to the vet.
Gus gets his check-up
and his shot.
Gus is sad at the vet's.

Bugs to Catch

Chapter 1: Kim and Pam

Kim and Pam have a job.
They check the grass
for bugs.

They prod and press
the grass.
They check for grubs
on the grass.

Kim and Pam
can spot the bugs,
but they cannot catch them.
Kim and Pam
are not quick to catch bugs.

Chapter 2: The Frog

A frog sits in the grass.
He catches bugs
in the grass.

Flick, flick!
The frog is as quick
as a flash.

The frog grabs bugs
and grins.
Yum! Yum!
The frog crams in
lots of bugs.

The frog is quick
to catch bugs.